The Best Of Enya

ISBN 0-7935-4717-2

HAL•LEONARD™ CORPORATION

7777 W. BLUEMOUND RD. P.O. BOX 13819 MILWAUKEE, WI 53213

AFER VENTUS

Written by ROMA RYAN
Composed and Arranged by
ENYA and NICKY RYAN

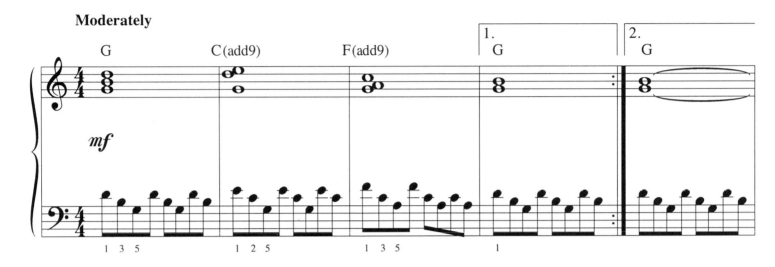

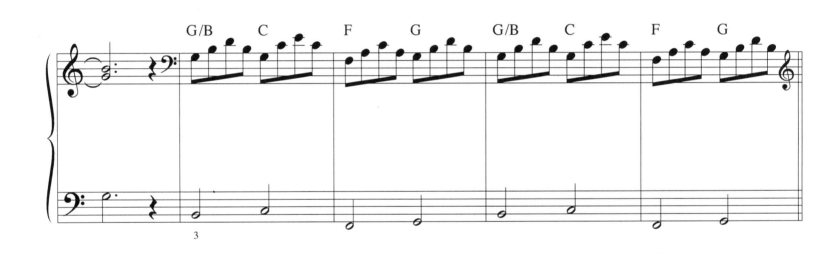

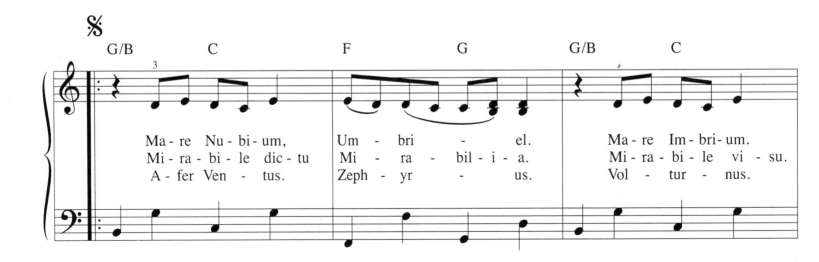

Mare Nubi-um, Um-bri- el. Mare Imbri-um.
Mi-ra-bi-le dic-tu Mi-ra-bil-i-a. Mi-ra-bi-le vi-su.
A-fer Ven- tus. Zeph-yr- us. Vol-tur-nus.

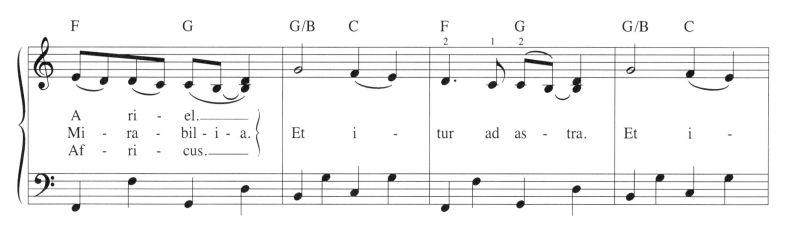

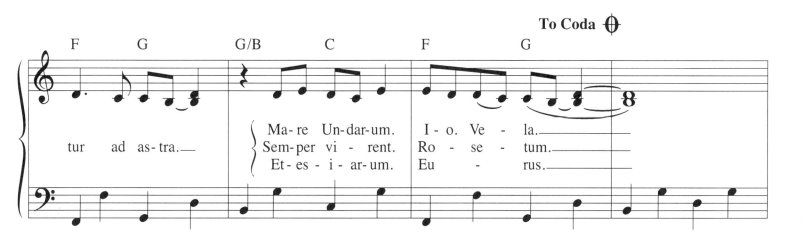

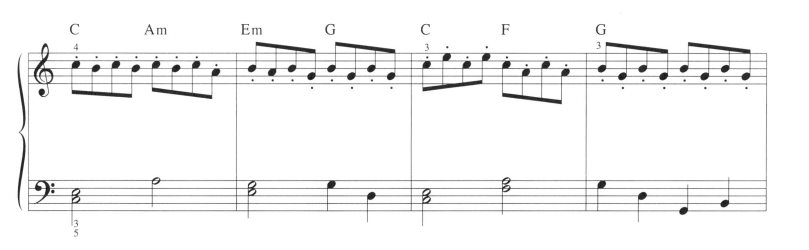

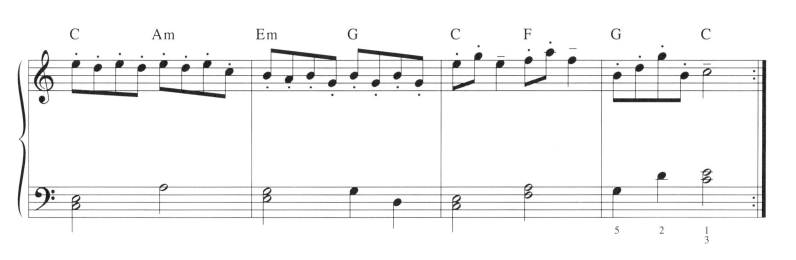

4

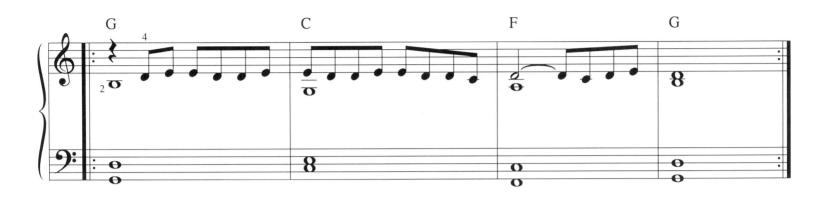

D.S. al Coda

CODA

Repeat and Fade

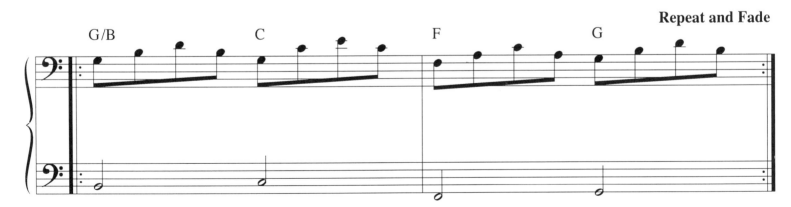

Running verse:

Suus cuique mos. Suum cuique.
Meus mihi, suus cuique carus.
Memento, terrigena.
Memento, vita brevis.
Meus mihi, suus cuique carus.

NO HOLLY FOR MISS QUINN

Composed and Arranged by
ENYA and NICKY RYAN

Slow and free

BOOK OF DAYS

Composed and Arranged by
ENYA and NICKY RYAN

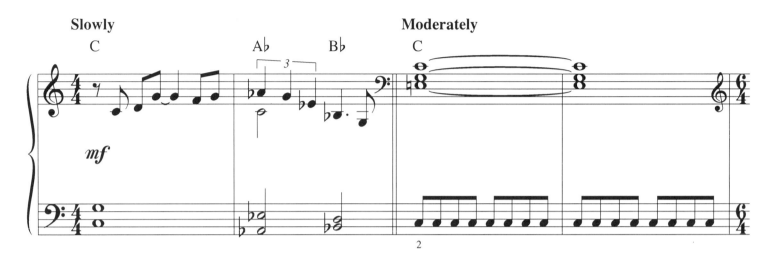

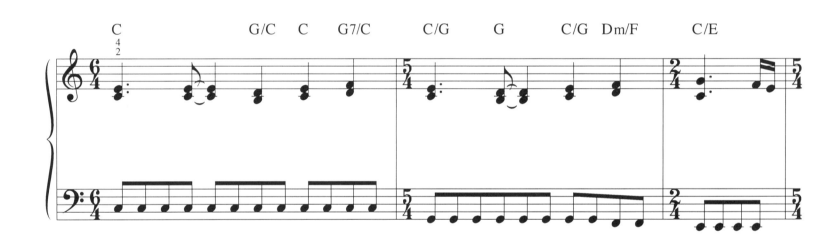

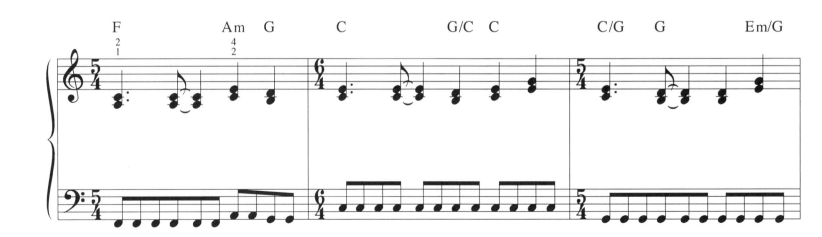

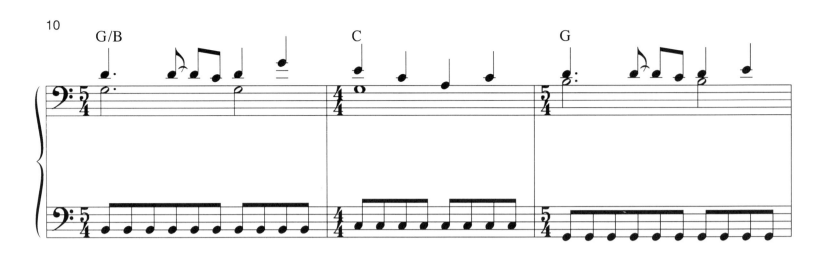

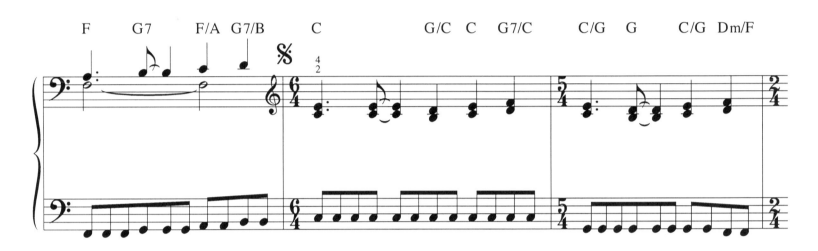

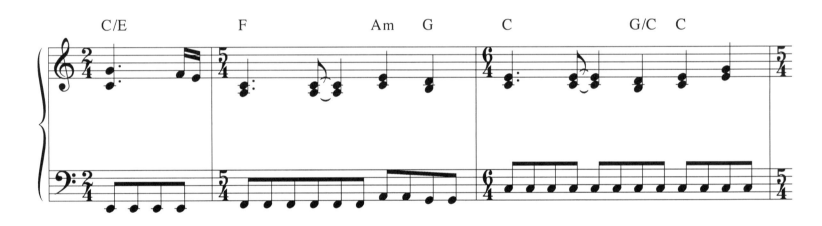

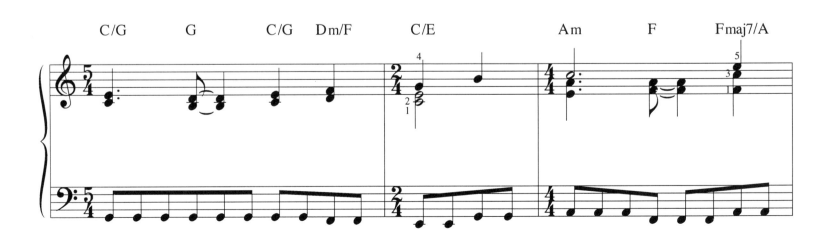

Ó oiche go hoích, mo thuras,
An bealach fada romhan.
Ó lá go lá, mo thuras,
na scéalta na mbeidh a choich.

CARIBBEAN BLUE

Composed and Arranged by
ENYA and NICKY RYAN

Quite fast

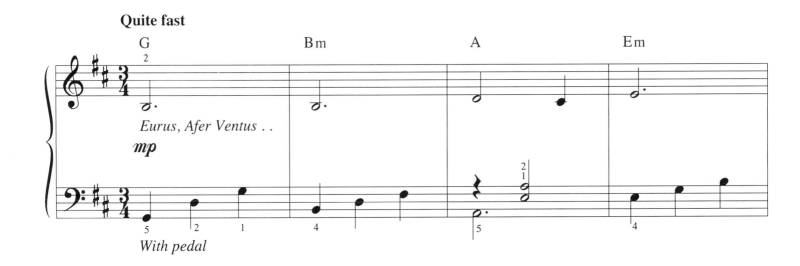

Eurus, Afer Ventus . .

With pedal

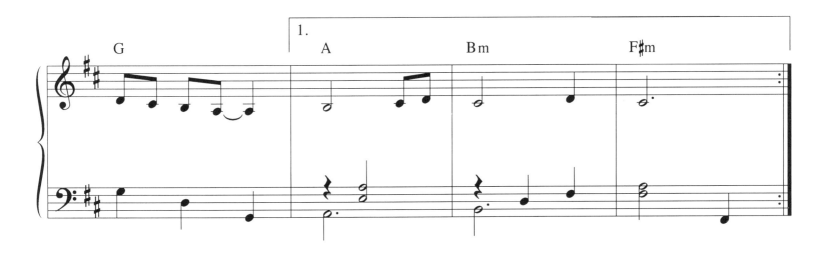

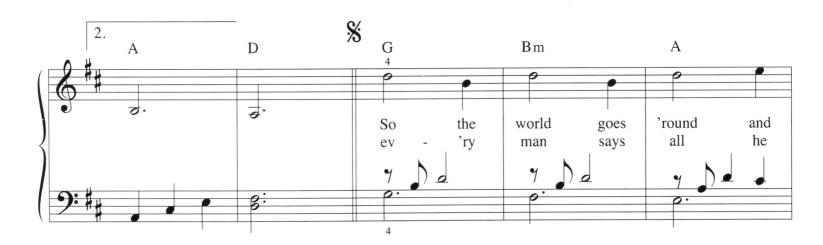

So the world goes 'round and
ev-'ry man says all and he

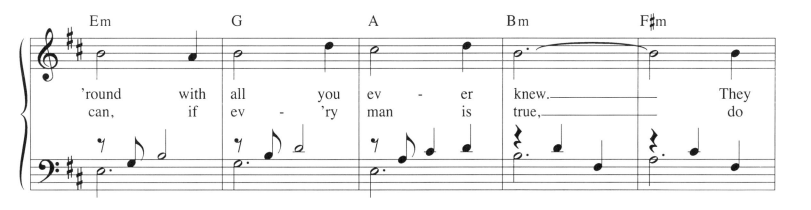

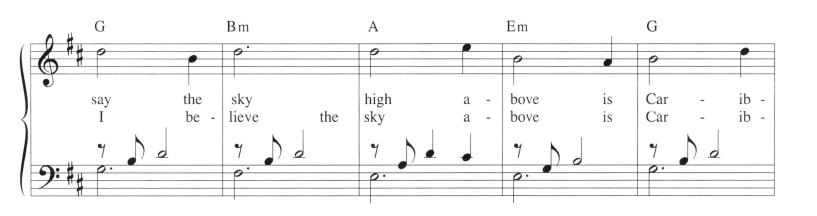

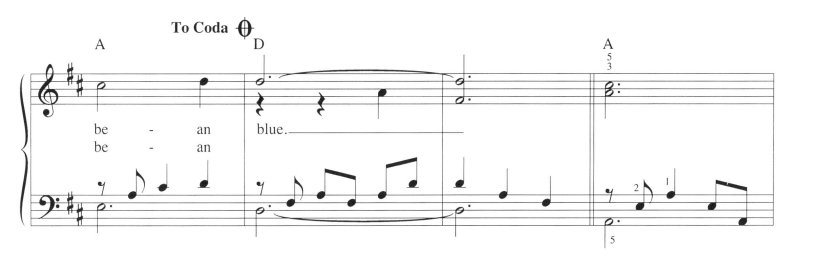

D.S. al Coda

If

CODA

blue.

Boreas, Zephyrus . . .

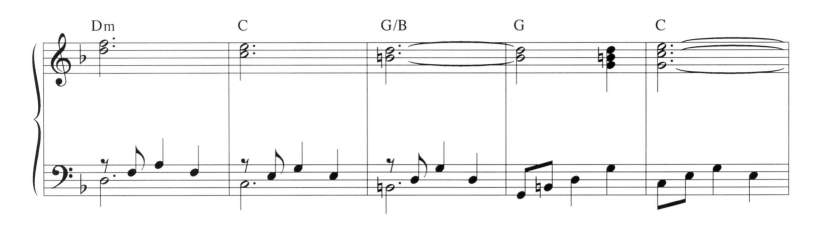

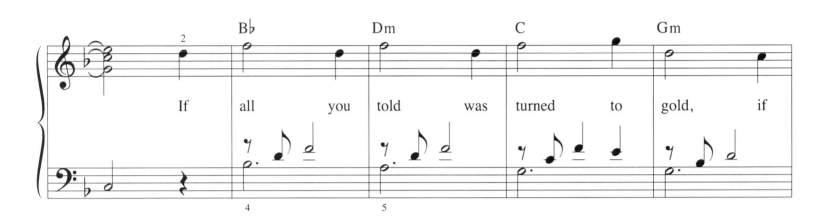

If all you told was turned to gold, if

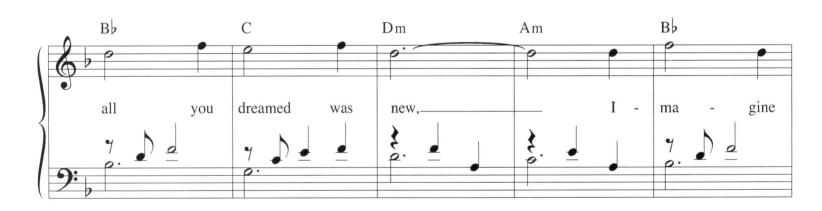

all you dreamed was new,_____ I - ma - gine

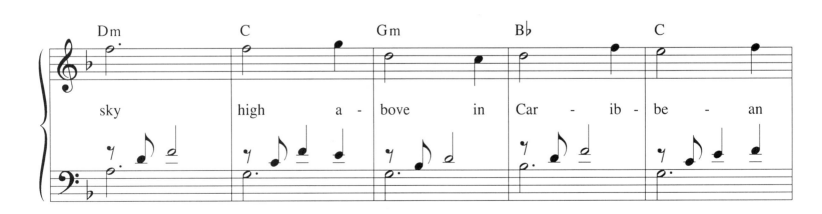

sky high a - bove in Car - ib - be - an

blue.

Eurus, Afer Ventus, Boreas Zephyrus, Africus . . .

THE CELTS

Written and Composed by ENYA,
NICKY RYAN and ROMA RYAN

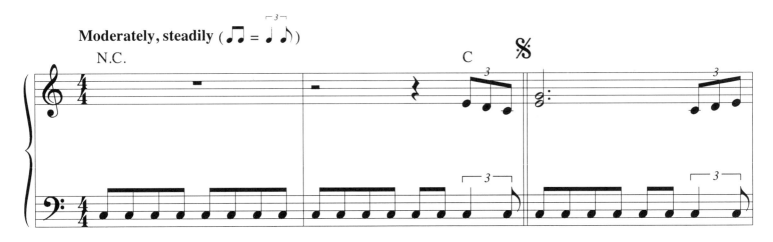

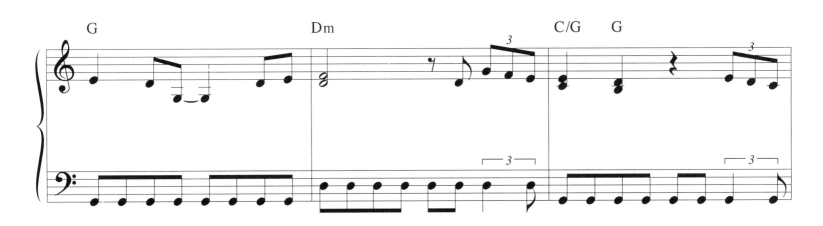

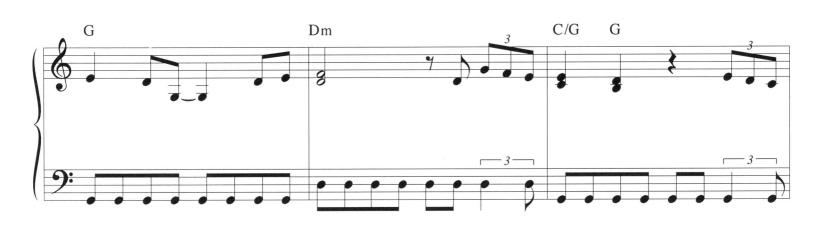

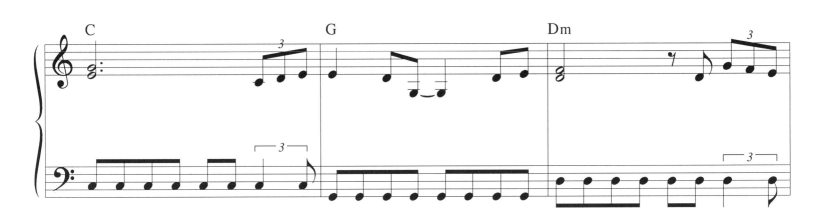

To Coda ⊕

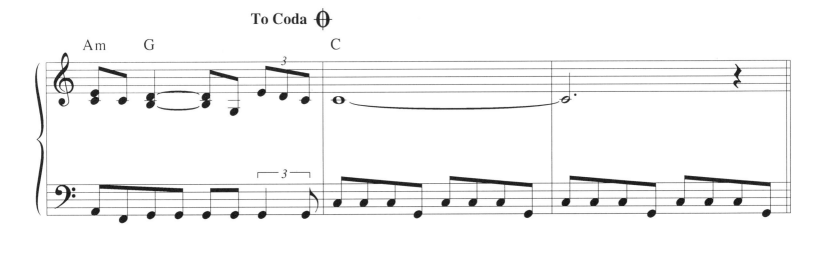

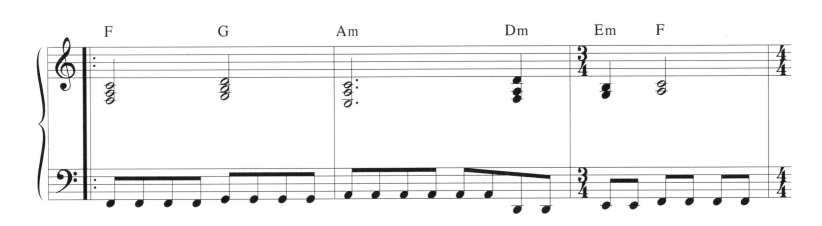

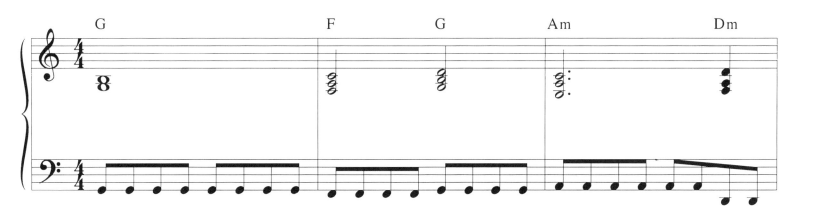

D.S. al Coda

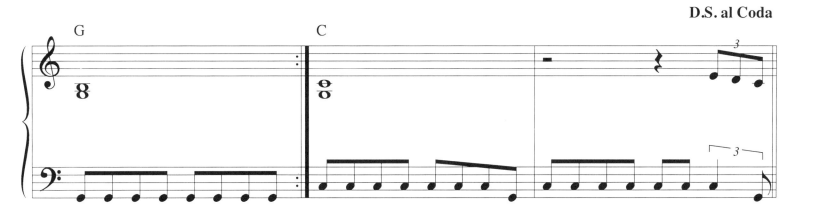

CODA

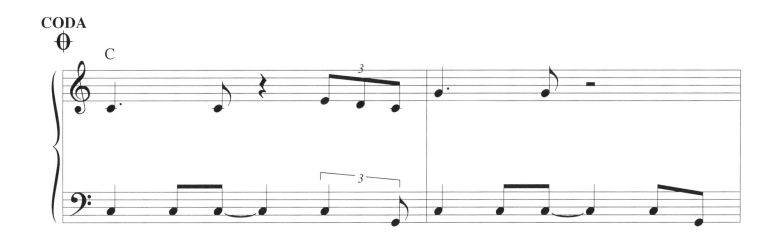

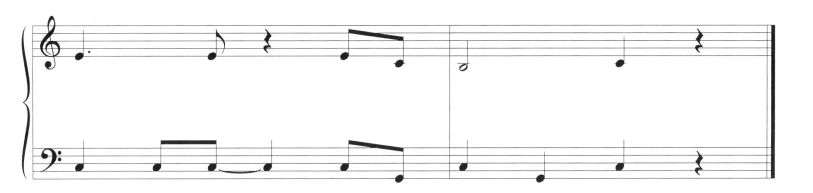

FAIRYTALE

Written and Composed by ENYA,
NICKY RYAN and ROMA RYAN

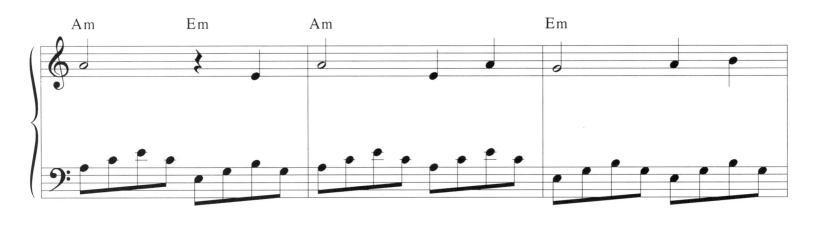

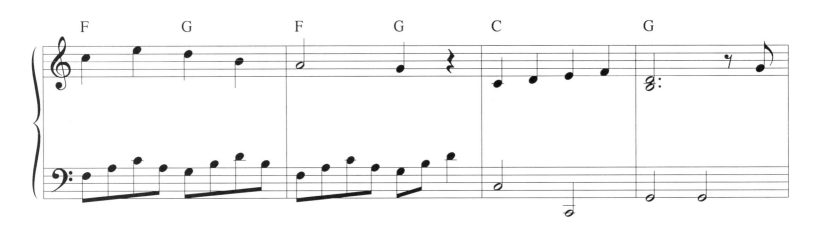

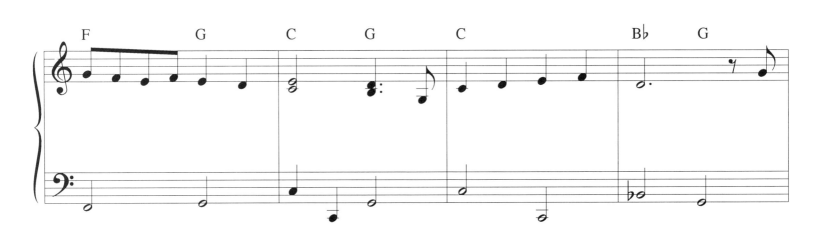

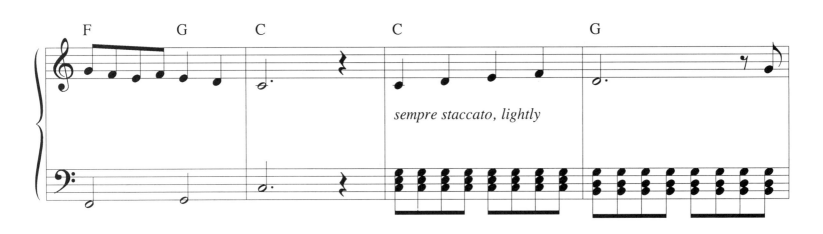

sempre staccato, lightly

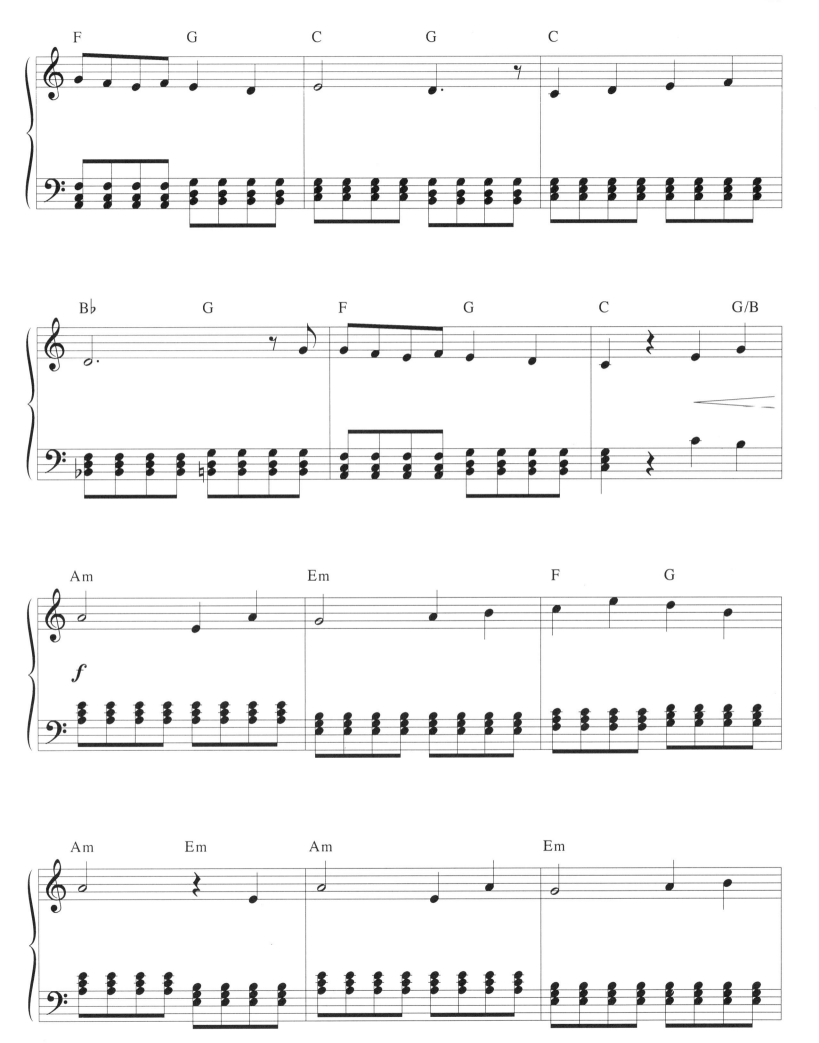

ORINOCO FLOW

Music by ENYA
Words by ROMA RYAN

Play cue note on repeat and D.S. only.

28

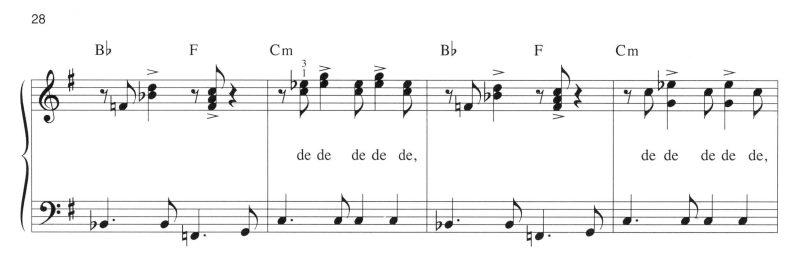

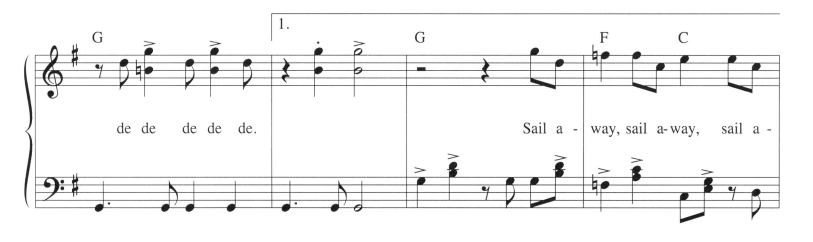

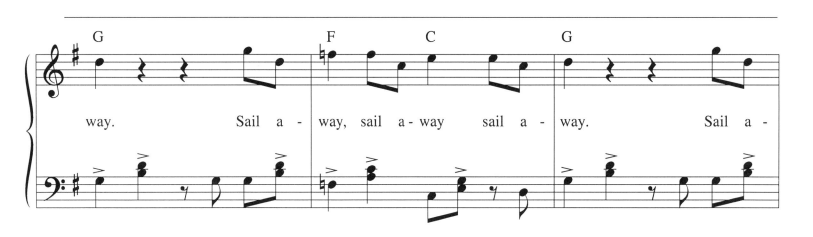

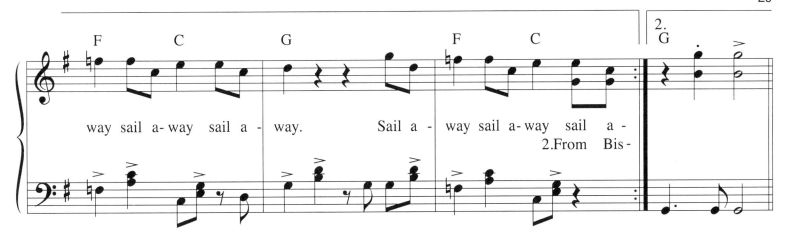

way sail a-way sail a - way. Sail a - way sail a-way sail a-

2.From Bis-

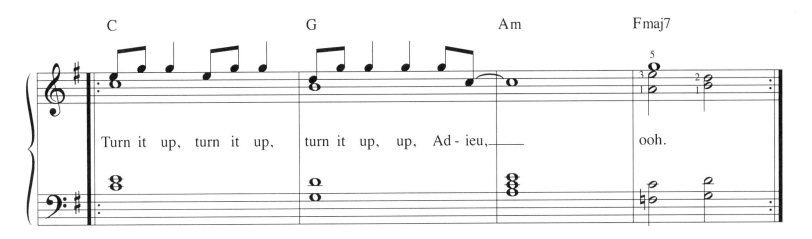

Turn it up, turn it up, turn it up, up, Ad - ieu,_____ ooh.

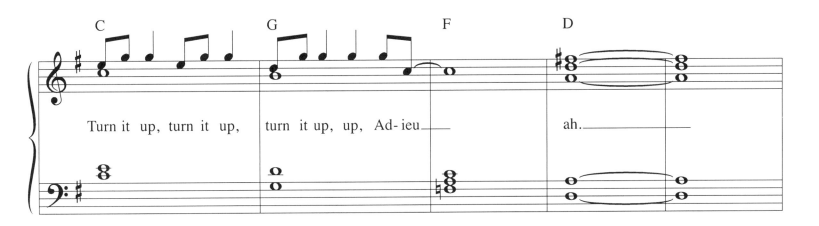

Turn it up, turn it up, turn it up, up, Ad-ieu___ ___ ah._____

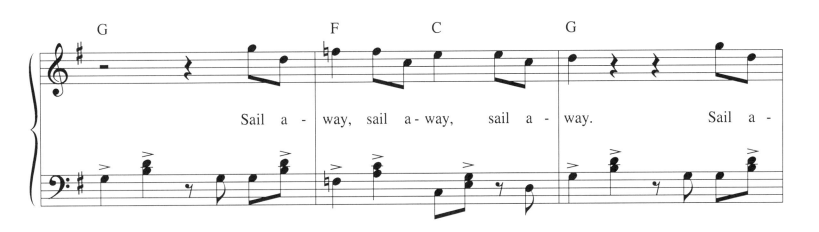

Sail a - way, sail a-way, sail a - way. Sail a-

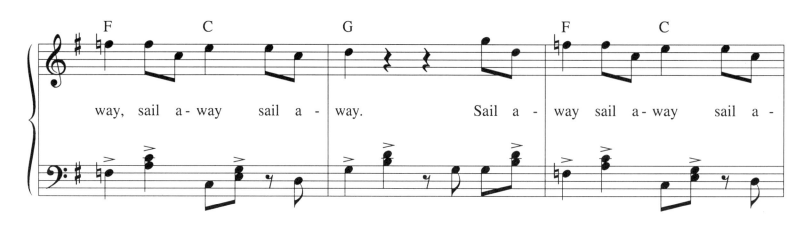

way, sail a-way sail a-way. Sail a-way sail a-way sail a-

D.S. al Coda

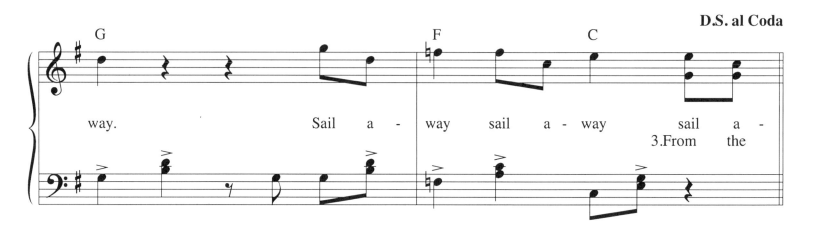

way. Sail a-way sail a-way sail a-
3.From the

CODA

lands I've ev-er seen. We can sail,__ we can sail,__ with the O-ri-no-co flow; we can

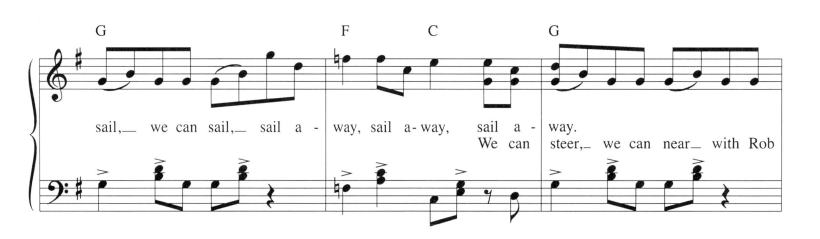

sail,__ we can sail,__ sail a-way, sail a-way, sail a-way.
We can steer,__ we can near__ with Rob

Dick-ins at the wheel,__ we can sigh,__ say good-bye__ Ross and his de-pen-den-cies. We can

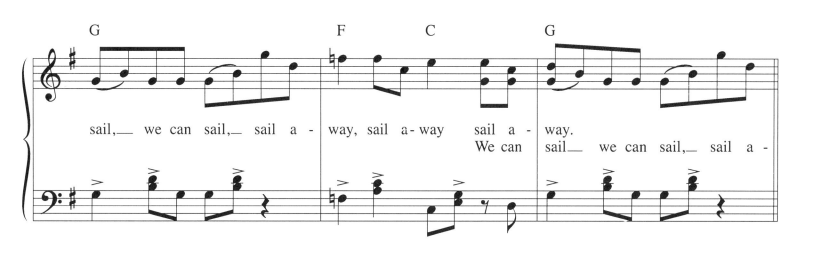

sail,__ we can sail,__ sail a - way, sail a-way sail a - way. We can sail__ we can sail,__ sail a -

Repeat and Fade

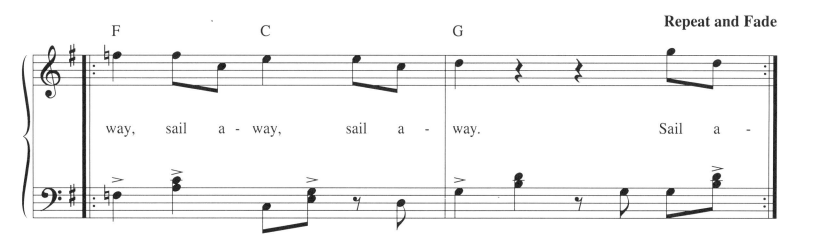

way, sail a - way, sail a - way. Sail a -

Additional Lyrics

From Bissau to Palau in the shade of Avalon
From Fiji to Tiree and the Isles of Ebony
From Peru to Cebu, feel the power of Babylon
From Bali to Cali far beneath the Coral Sea.

From the North to the South, Ebadae unto Khartoum
From the deep Sea of Clouds to the Island of the Moon
Carry me on the waves to the lands I've never been
Carry me on the waves to the lands I've never seen.

31

ON YOUR SHORE

Music by ENYA
Words by NICKY RYAN

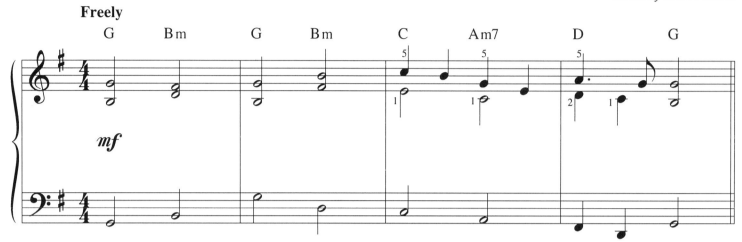

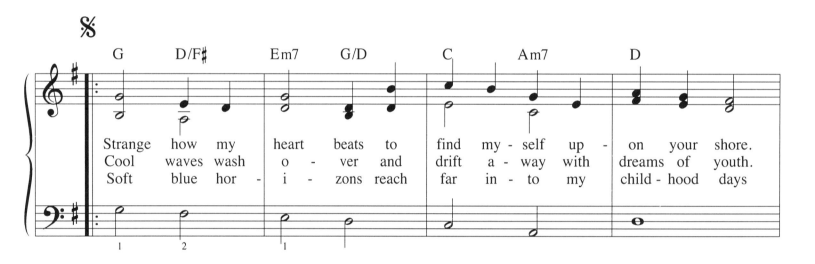

Strange how my heart beats to find my-self up-on your shore.
Cool waves wash o - ver and drift a - way with dreams of youth.
Soft blue hor - i - zons reach far in - to my child - hood days

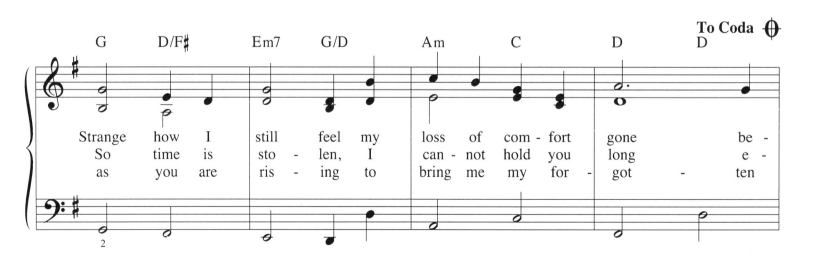

Strange how I still feel my loss of com - fort gone be -
So time is sto - len, I can - not hold you long e -
as you are ris - ing to bring me my for - got - ten

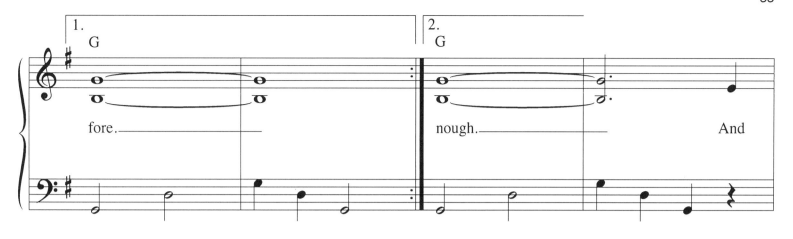

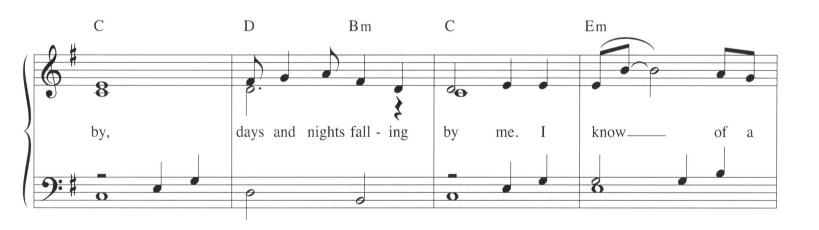

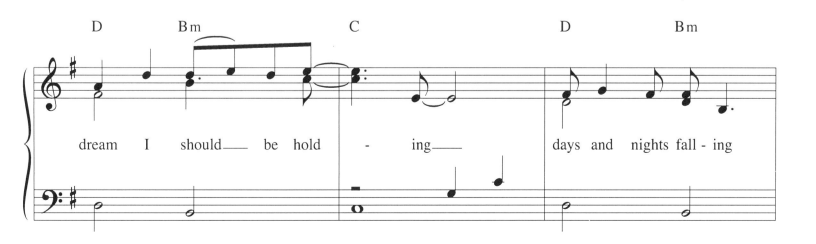

D.S. al Coda

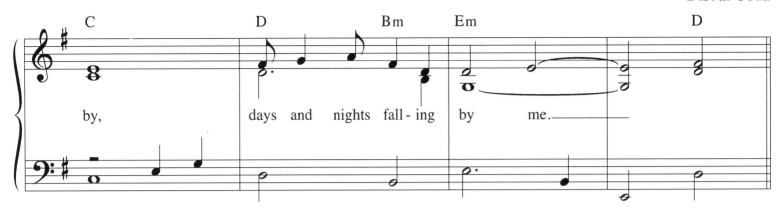

by,   days and nights fall-ing by   me.

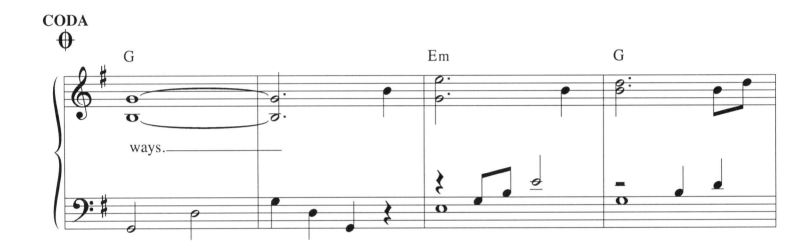

ways.

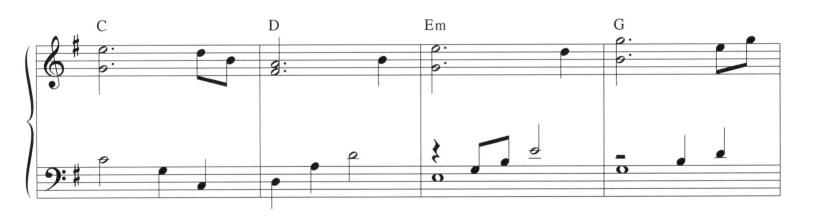

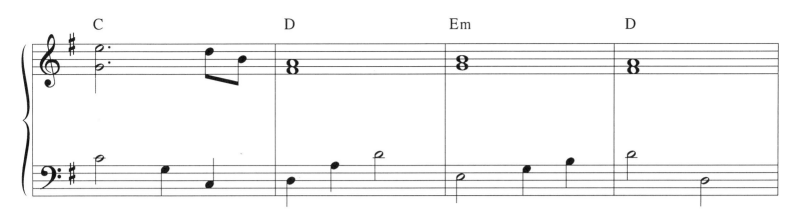

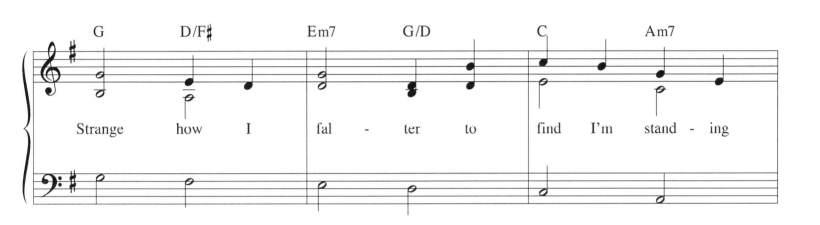

Strange how I fal - ter to find I'm stand - ing

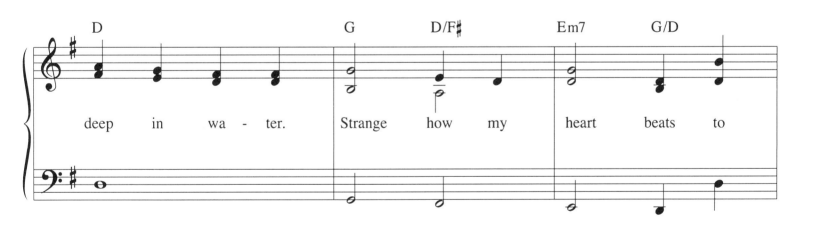

deep in wa - ter. Strange how my heart beats to

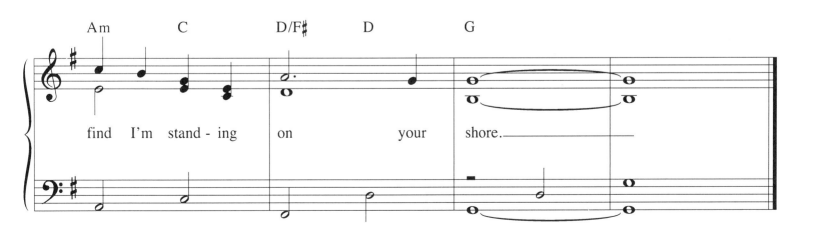

find I'm stand - ing on your shore.

SHEPHERD MOONS

Composed and Arranged by
ENYA and NICKY RYAN

STORMS IN AFRICA

Music by ENYA
Words by ROMA RYAN

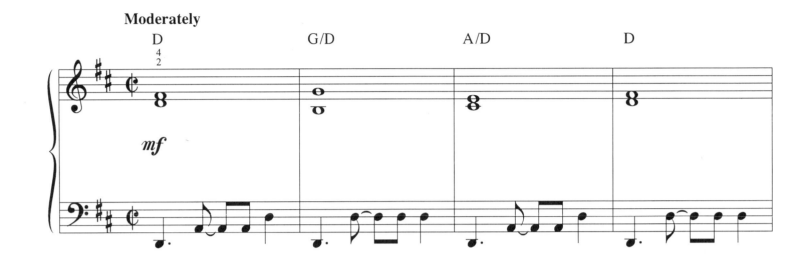

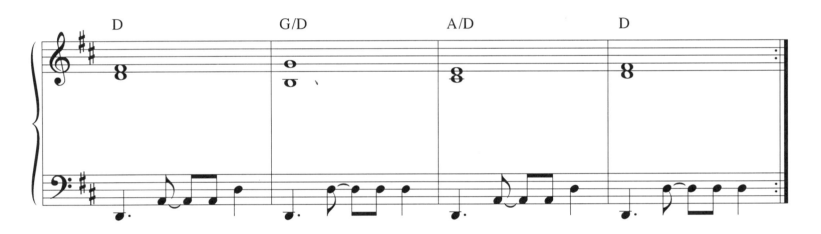

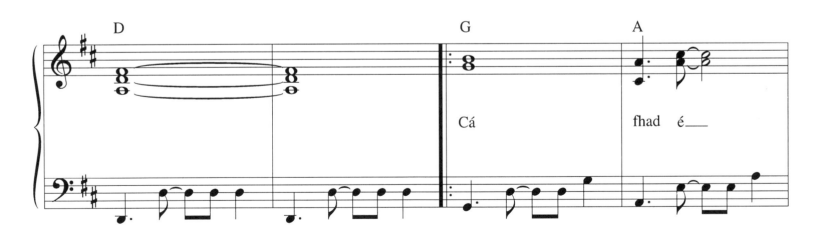

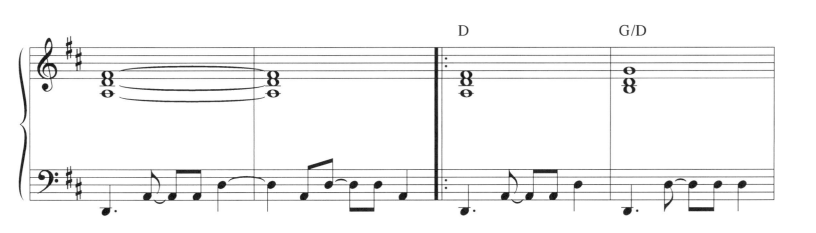

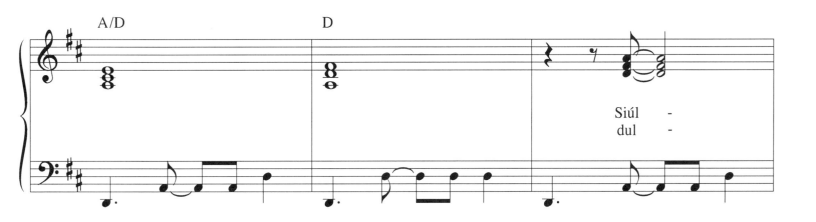

Siúl -
dul -

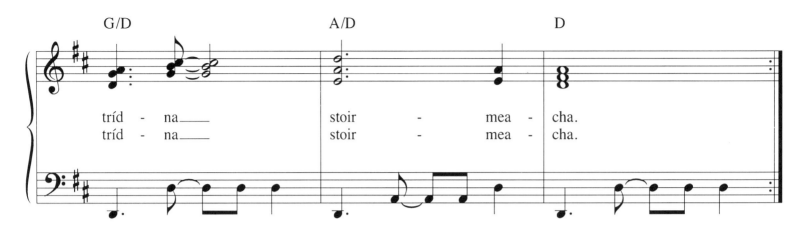

G/D ... **A/D** ... **D**

tríd - na____ stoir - mea - cha.
tríd - na____ stoir - mea - cha.

D ... **G**

Cá

A ... **Bm** ... **G**

fhad é____ ó an tús

A7 ... **D** ... **G**

don stoirm. Cá

fhad é___ ó an tús

go deir - eadh.___

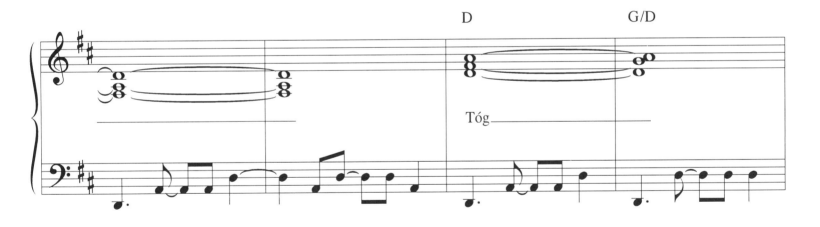

Tóg___

do chroí_ súil_ tríd - na___

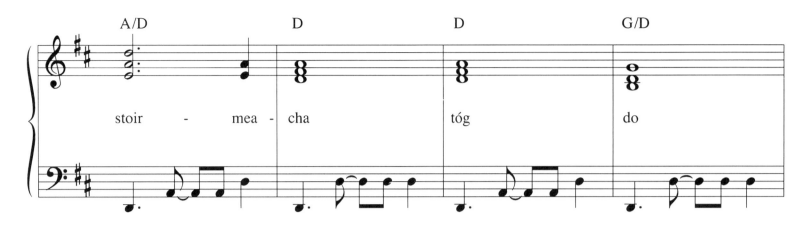

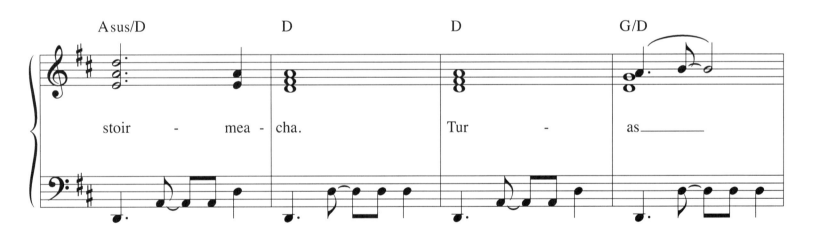

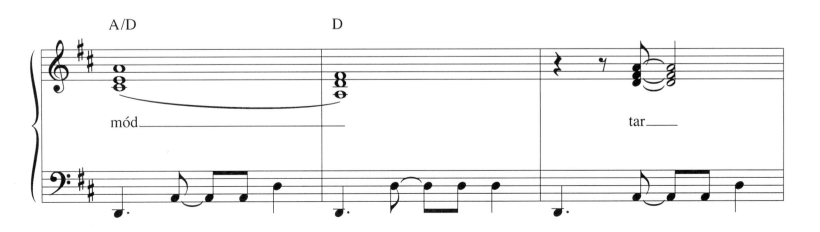

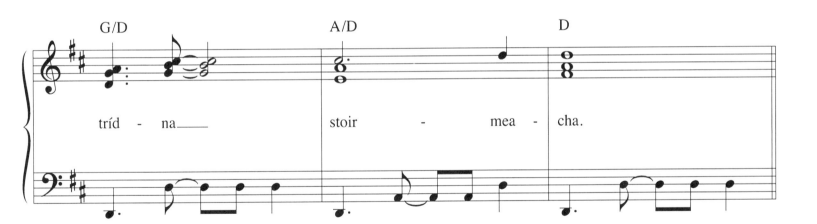

Repeat and Fade

TO GO BEYOND

Written and Composed by ENYA,
NICKY RYAN and ROMA RYAN

WATERMARK

Music by ENYA
Words by ROMA RYAN

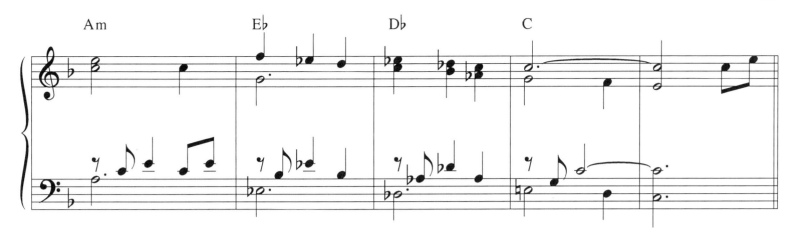

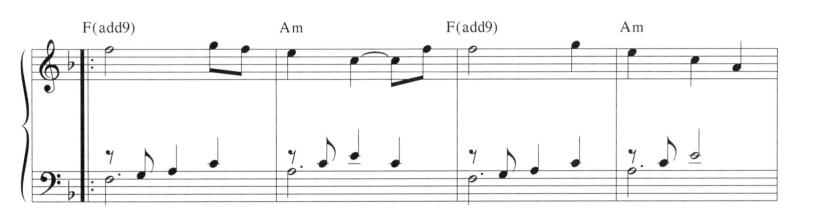

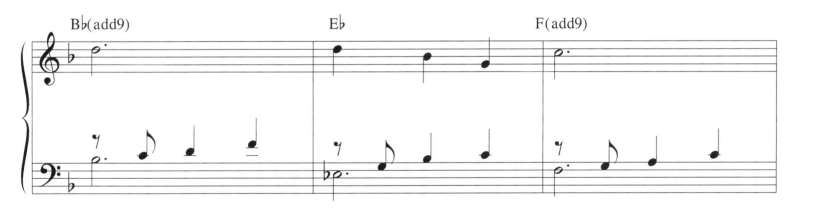

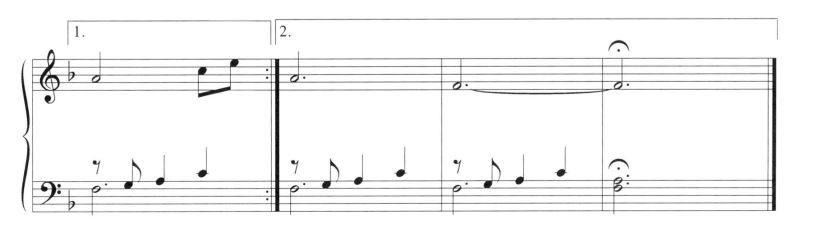